for grandpa johnny and grandma on the farm

A FAMILY OF DREAMERS

A FAMILY OF DREAMERS

POEMS

SAMANTHA NOCK

TALONBOOKS

Talonbooks
9259 Shaughnessy Street, Vancouver, British Columbia, Canada V6P 6R4
talonbooks.com

Talonbooks is located on xʷməθkʷəy̓əm, Sḵwx̱wú7mesh, and səlilwətaɬ Lands.

First printing: 2023

Typeset in Arno
Printed and bound in Canada on 100% post-consumer recycled paper

Cover and interior design by Leslie Smith
Cover image by Leslie Smith

Talonbooks acknowledges the financial support of the Canada Council for the Arts, the Government of Canada through the Canada Book Fund, and the Province of British Columbia through the British Columbia Arts Council and the Book Publishing Tax Credit.

Canada   Canada Council   Conseil des arts   BRITISH   BRITISH COLUMBIA
          for the Arts   du Canada   COLUMBIA   ARTS COUNCIL
                                                            An agency of the Province of British Columbia

Library and Archives Canada Cataloguing in Publication

Title: A family of dreamers : poems / Samantha Nock.
Names: Nock, Samantha, author.
Description: Includes bibliographical references.
Identifiers: Canadiana 20230466974 | ISBN 9781772015478 (softcover)
Subjects: LCGFT: Poetry.
Classification: LCC PS8627.O28 F36 2023 | DDC C811/.6—dc23

my aunty says
I am a daughter
a daughter for all.

—RITA BOUVIER
"I say I am," *papîyâhtak* (2004)

piyak

a brief celebration

sam, m'girl, remember they don't understand
what it's like to live in this body.

this is a reminder
to stop trying to leave
before they leave you.

your body is used to daily little hurts.
she has learned to swallow it,
blink away the tears,
and move on.

maybe this is coping,
maybe this is caging yourself,
within your own bones.

sam, please remember
that you're not just a house
built of grief.

this body is song,
it is poetry.

you are not a secret
whispered into your own mouth.

m'girl,
you are sweetgrass
and riverbeds.

sammy baby girl,
hold your own hands.
you need to trust
that in the morning
you will still be here.

you're built of dreamers,
with one finger
pointing to the exit.

you can't outrun yourself, sam
let yourself go
you have plenty of time.

m'girl,
you will never
and should never be
enough for anyone but yourself
you need to stop
cutting down your own trees
to build a home for someone else.

they will come and they will go,
you can't hold onto someone's spirit,
if it's already halfway out the door – sam,
sometimes the letting go comes at the beginning.

sammy baby girl,
this life is a brief celebration.

letting go

the act of letting go comes in three parts with
an epilogue and a prologue.

the prologue is simple and not simple at all. the
prologue is stories that aren't my stories to tell.
it's a halfbreed baby girl born during k'sîpîsim,
the cold moon.

my dad tells me my first words were:
"what's that?"

part one is an act of seeing and unseeing the
same thing over and over.

over and over, i remember images of northern
prairie fields of canola driving from dawson
to pouce.

remember teen years and late nights.
remember sneaking out to parties. remember
smoking my first cigarette, mouth moving to
hand instead of hand to mouth. over and over,
mixed with memories of grandma showing me
johnny-jump-ups in her yard: small, purple,
and stubborn. over and over, remember pulling
chickweed from her flower beds, over and over,
remember how it felt to dip my small child
hands in red peace-country clay. over and over,
remember grandpa skinning martin from the
trapline. over and over, making the promise
that i would learn to set snares.

grief like guilt, it comes, over and over.

part two is a never-ending movie with jump
cuts. the optics of me wearing my dad's ties
and shirts in middle school. short black hair
and eyeliner to the top of my cheeks. one foot
in the river and one foot on the road. it's going
to kokum's to sit beside her on her couch as
she watches *the young and the restless*. to listen
to her, my aunty, and my mom talk about "that
damn victor." it's riding horses while dreaming
of what it would be like to steal that horse
and run away. it's watching him put snoose
in his lip, and remembering how much i hate
him. it's listening to "dreams" by fleetwood
mac on cassette on a small yellow walkman. i
apologize to horses because i know i'm leaving
that summer. fleet is the first to know of my
plans. it's feeling the grass tickle me as i sit and
wonder what it's going to be like. it's feeling 13
and 45 at the same time. the scene playing out
from two different viewpoints, varying only
slightly.

a change comes in part three.
working hard in high school because i'm a
cliché of wanting to leave my small town. it's
following in my big brother's footsteps. it's
learning to leave my own. it comes with trading
canola for coastal waters, leaving summer
thunderstorms and driving down country
roads in my ford ranger. it's saying goodbye

to the lands that raised me. it's knowing that, when i left at 13 and he said "you can never come back," he was wrong.

it's knowing he's right.

sometimes change comes all at once and sometimes so slowly it feels like it's not happening at all. it's being a small fish in a big pond and imposter syndrome in every university class. it's finding comfort in the faces of the ndns i meet in those classes. they remind me of home and *the young and the restless*. and that damn victor.

there is an everlasting epilogue.

it's the three women that raised me coming together to make the sick one tea. it's being a thousand miles away hoping tea is the cure. it's feeling so small next to cedar. the ending is making family out of more than blood. making friends out of lovers and lovers out of friends. it's wondering if i'll ever lose this feeling in the pit of my stomach. it's the time i fell into the moberly and thought i was drowning. my body took over to swim us back to shore. it's looking back, exhausted and panting, to see the ghost of myself sinking to the bottom of the lake.

transference

i fell in love with my therapist.

or at least fell in love with freely
telling someone my deepest parts,
the ones i've carefully hidden behind jokes.
jokes make people feel comfortable
with the ways i've learned to haphazardly put
myself back together.

it's halfbreed tradition, you know –
to open your wounds and let the laughter
drip out.

we talk in coded words.

together we never say things like:
- anxiety disorder
- depression
- disorganized attachment disorder
- complex post-traumatic stress disorder

instead, i tell her the parts of my body where
these entities live.

they hide in the pit of my stomach
live in the space between my shoulder blades
where my birthmark sits.

once i read that birthmarks are scars from our
past lives.

aunty says i am an old soul,
i wonder how many lives i've lived before?
it feels like i'm new on this earth, but
some days it feels like i've danced her into being.

there's no guidebook on how you tell people
you are a host to poltergeists.

we use metaphors to talk about disassociation:
i am a ghost looking back at myself.

is there a way to learn to love your traumas?
maybe we could make one happy family.

they gift me with knowledge
passed down from one generation to the next.

you can call it hypervigilance but my instincts
are almost always right.

my body and her guests
have taught me how to survive
and that is a beautiful thing.

sometimes she's an unreliable narrator,
telling me danger is around every corner

we negotiate constantly
for territory.

whispering in my ear when it's time to go,
she says:
"cut your losses, m'girl"

i have to tell my body
that no matter where we run
we will always be together.

i am sovereign territory
that i share in treaty with
these accidental and terrible gifts.

dawson creek,

i was born in your small hospital
returned to your flat dusty streets in adolescence.
i have written and deleted so many lines of
poetry for you,
you were the first place i loved and left.

home

let's undress these wounds.

let's walk for miles.

it's okay to not know where
the kîskatinâw meets the peace
but understand that i exist
by dipping my feet in both rivers
and eating berries from the bushes
that grow on their banks.

i am here, whole and lonely
deeply indebted to myself
and the earth
i crawled out of.

kîskatinâw interlude pt. I

for the kîskatinâw river and all the stories she holds

if you use the palms of your hands
to caress the muddy banks of the kîskatinâw
let your fingers slip through her silt
that is what i imagine it feels like to hold me.
this is what it feels like to be there and not at
the same time.

the kîskatinâw looks like she runs slow,
eases around river bends,
has shallow warm pools
that will hold your body.
kîskatinâw means "cutbank" in my language,
it means get too close to the edge
and you will fall in.

i wonder what it feels like to be both a mighty
and tender thing?

the river never has to apologize for the space
she takes up
wide shores hold life.
deep water cuts away at rock.
pulls trees into her arms by their roots.
she is so gentle in parts
and so vicious in others.
enter at the wrong place
and she will bring you down
into her depths. ·

more than human

i bloody my knuckles
punching the tough crusted snow
of my homelands.

watch the pink snow melt into streams:
please carry my heavy spirit to the ocean.

miyösin mîna piyakwâw î wâpamtân,
what is it like to trust that prairie crocuses will
stick their weary heads through the frost
every spring?

the rocks sewn into my stomach
make relaxing into soft grass impossible
the fresh-faced forget-me-nots keeping asking,
"nimwî cî nân'taw kitisâyân?"

i keep asking the chokecherries
to remind me why they love me,
"ôta cî nikî nihtâwikin?"

i shake the red berries from their branches
hoping they will fall into my hands in tender ways.

the problem with shaking berries from their roots
is that eventually no berries will be left to shake.

i ask the paper birch:
"mwîstas kakî wâpam'tin?"
please wrap me in your soft bark
i want to be enveloped, fully.

pull me into your firm trunk and swallow me whole.

together, birch tree,
we can listen to the wind celebrate our skins
as it blows through our leaves every summer.

what an existence it is to be:
daughter and sister to all these things,
solitary and held in their roots and waters.

i can't pull at their tender pedicles,
asking if i'll be okay.

the melting snow unearthing fall rot
fertilizes the spring growth,
as it blooms into late-summer harvest,
reminds me what will always be.

we have to let our dead leaves fall
to grow a stronger tree.

wayfinding

"i'm almost there, six stops away"

Commercial.
McLean.
Clark.
Glen.
Campbell.
Hawks.

i'm minutes away from where the blood mixes,
where i'm going to spend the next four hours
exploring the shapes of acquaintances, beer,
and cigarettes.

if i close my eyes
i can picture the road to grandma's house:

head down 97N, turn left at the cemetery, go
a few klicks past ted's service, left again at the
tumbler ridge turnoff, hang a right at the sound
barrier fence my grandpa built four summers
ago so my grandma wouldn't have to listen
to the jake brake squeals of the trucks going
down the highway

follow the loop of their drive, past sheds with
snares hanging on the door with bear skins
nailed on the side. park in front of the house
my grandpa made with logs of wood cut from
down the road. follow the path where i used to
dig up red clay with rusty tonka trucks.

to say goodbye, honk the horn and look back:
grandma will be waving in the window

follow cracked sidewalks to sit on the back steps
talk about the ways in which these
nights feel real and surreal.

i am rooted here.

even though i can still draw a map to the field where
wild strawberries grow in the summertime

i don't believe in in-between spaces.
i don't believe in long-winded monologues
about walking in two worlds

my existence isn't reconciling
the changing seasons
with the way
i count time by bus stops.

nîso

on the farm,

i am free.

crabgrass brushes against my knuckles,
cold pond water runs through my fingers.

a make-believe world between spruce trees,
this is where i begin: again, and again, and
again.

tell me a story, let's play pictionary, let's drink
one more cup of coffee.

i would give everything
for just one more cup of coffee
with you.

grandma-on-the-farm

sometimes grandma
i wonder if i grieved you right.

your hands pulling up chickweed,
making popsicle-stick cabins,
teaching me how to embroider hummingbirds
and delicate pink roses
onto white cotton.

on the farm with you,
my safe place is your kitchen table
playing card game after card game
till six o'clock and grandpa's home.

eating moose meat and gravy over mashed
potatoes and a slice of white bread with
margarine.

i wonder if you know
why i never said goodbye.

grandma, i am scared of my own grief.
i hide a thousand miles away,
making excuses.

when i hear the cranberries or loretta lynn or
dolly parton, i think of you.

i know love isn't
measured in time
or goodbyes

but a moment never passes
without you
and your trees
on my mind.

there's no way to hold this grief
it never ends
it sits in my lungs
and tightens them.

when i close my eyes,
i can picture the late-afternoon sunlight
falling through the windows
while we watch taped reruns of
all my children.

i see you in every chickadee
and hear you every time
they sing to us:
"spring's here."

a cup of black coffee, noodle soup, a cheese
sandwich, a slice of apple pie for dessert, and a
can of warm coke.

you made the darkest parts of growing up the
brightest.

i will always look back
to see if you're waving goodbye.

grandpa-on-the-farm

grandpa's hands are rough from farm work.
fingers calloused from making truck springs all
day.

he runs his bent fingers over the back of his old
bay saddle horse and says,
"one summer we will go riding."

i promise him i will, and maybe it won't
happen but the promise of a promise is enough
for the both of us.

we walk through the bush
spending most of our time in silence
teaching me that some conversations aren't
about talking.

he points out where young bull moose scratch
the velvet off their antlers,
tells me how to find my way home if i'm ever
lost in the woods,
tells me what berries to eat.

he says that nightshade is poisonous.

every night after dinner, grandpa gets up from
the table. puts on his cowboy hat and plaid
jacket, slips on his boots. without saying a
word, walks out the door.

he comes back to watch *jeopardy!* and answers
every question right,
drinks his last cup of coffee, catches the news,
and goes to bed.

when i was a kid i took it upon myself to raise
tadpoles in a little pond out the front of my
grandparents' house.

it's "sam's pond."

one hot summer, the pond dried up and the
tadpoles were drying up too.
bucket by bucket, we carried them to his
rainwater barrel.

my dad and him knew they weren't going to
make it, and between the tears,
i did too.

but he helped me carry dead tadpoles to fresh
water anyway.

miyo iskwew

for all my mothers

kokum, what does it mean to be a
"good woman"?
i have watched your small hands knead
bannock in the bowl
flatten it and put it in the oven to bake
stir hangover soup and boil neck bones
salt the meat and pull small flecks off to eat.

grandma, you taught me to slow down.
listen to chickadees call us into spring
watch for hummingbirds on a quiet afternoon
and embroider pink roses on white cloth, while
you talk about your plans for the next hunting
season.

mom, i love you to the moon and back.
i have watched you drive hundreds of miles,
and i'll be with you to drive hundreds more.

when grandma on the farm got sick,
i was a thousand miles away.

mom and kokum show up at her house,
sit around the kitchen table and drink coffee
and smoke cigarettes.
the three women that dreamed me into being,
come together.

mom and kokum teach grandpa how to brew
the chaga and bear-root tea,
and to add the rat root with honey.

my mom calls me after,
she hopes this will help.

the thought of them brewing old knowledge
to cure cancer breaks me wide open.

grandma passes away that winter.
i miss the funeral,
still and always
a thousand miles away.

the three women that formed me out of
tough love,
old country songs,
and huckleberries,
have lost one of their own.

that night i don't cry until grandma visits and
tells me:
"don't worry, be happy."

fort st. john,

i remember when there used to be nothing
but flat fields in front of my elementary school.

behind kokum's house,
i play pretend in the backyard.
climb on the railing of the porch and talk to
the ravens.

ki miyokîsikan'sin, babe?

the lord's prayer

when we stayed at kokum's she'd tuck us into
sleep and say the lord's prayer. leaning over the
back of the couch, the same couch i fell off of
as a toddler and broke my nose, she'd start:

our father who art in heaven

plagued by nightmares, each passing pile of
clothes or a coat hanging on the chair was a
threat, a monster, some horror hiding in the
corner. they'd seep into my dreams.

hallowed be thy name

kokum's house smelled like garlic, bread, white
diamonds perfume, grandpa, and must. the
couch i slept on, kokum's couch, was small
with a cushion worn down where she sat. this
was her spot, and i am the lucky one that gets
to sleep on her couch.

thy kingdom come

my brother slept less than five feet away on
the bigger couch, the one that grandpa would
sometimes sit on to watch the news. but
grandpa spent his days in the chair on the far
side of the kitchen table. playing one long
game of solitaire, drinking iced tea out of a
plastic measuring cup. eating pickled herring
or pickled eggs or boiling a pot of pork hocks.

thy will be done on earth, as it is in heaven

the day grandpa's spirit returned home, mom
called me at 7 a.m. (phone calls before 8 a.m.
and after 11 p.m. are never good). as she told
me, i didn't react. i hung up and journeyed
back in to the dreamworld. a nightmare held
me. i woke up L and cried. we bought beer, a
pack of cigarettes, and sat in the park before my
flight home.

give us this day our daily bread

when i walked through the door of
kokum's house, it was full of family.
i couldn't look at the kitchen table.
couldn't look at
the worn-down spot on the tablecloth.
couldn't look at
the ratty deck of cards sitting there untouched.
kokum was sitting in her spot, watching tv.
"hi babe," she said, not meeting my eyes.

none of us cried.

and forgive us our trespasses

we spent the week preparing for his feast.
cabbage rolls, bannock, potato salad, to be
eaten at the friendship centre. cree prayer
before english prayer. this was as much for
kokum as it was for grandpa. we get home
and kokum sits opposite to where grandpa

sat, grabs the ratty deck of cards: small brown
hands shuffling and reshuffling grief.

she starts a game of solitaire.

as we forgive those who trespass against us

she looks up from her game and asks,
"who will i fight with now?"

and lead us not into temptation

a month later i had my first experience of sleep
paralysis. i lie in my bed and see something
standing in the corner. i am scared and can't
move, can't scream. this is the dreamworld
entering the waking world, i know this is grief
coming to collect. covered in sweat, heart
beating, the thing is no longer in the corner of
my room but now i sleep with the lights on.

but deliver us from evil

last week grandma on the farm took the same
journey as grandpa.
a nightmare greets me every night and
i wonder how many days i can stay awake.

kokum says we come from a family of
dreamers.

amen.

n'sto

âstam

for lindsay m, the biggest brat

come here,
apitân.

it's wintertime now
we can tell stories.

the spirits are resting
they won't follow us home.

tell me yours.

rest your head on my lap.
i'll braid your hair like wihkwaskwa.

you understand
how hard it is
when your mother
and grandmother
and great-grandmother
have all been taught that
being vulnerable
has never ended well for us.

but for you,
i'll try.

âstam.
now tell me,
how did it hurt?

they don't understand
how much we brawl and clash
and fight with nails and teeth
only to get told
that we didn't fight hard enough
that we didn't do enough
to someone doing enough to us.

you don't have to bite your way out.
anymore.

they don't know how to read the stars,

but we do.

the spirits in our bodies tell us
that when we can no longer speak
they will speak for us.

it wasn't me who set the world on fire
it was our great-grandmothers' hands
that lit the match
and let it go.

âstam.
rest your head on my lap,
close your eyes,

let's watch them burn.

my body of muskeg

when you're in the bush
look for dead spruce,
grey and leaning sideways
that's where the muskeg is.

i'm waiting for the bus on renfrew,
it's bringing me to the final witnessing event.
today, i'm supposed to heal
enough for my family.

muskeg will swallow a human whole.
moose sink to the bottom,
so i'm told
so i tell people from the city.

"i'm going to listen
to speakers and survivors
from that system
you survived,"
i tell kokum on the phone.

permafrost doesn't let
the water through
it doesn't let the decomposing
wood and bugs and spirits through.

"find me answers, babe"
she orders me from the other end.

she wasn't allowed to heal
with this so-called nation.

her story isn't big enough
to be in the sad chapter
of this country's history.

moss covers
mud
covers
unknown beings
below the surface.

i listen to white talking heads
talk about
reconciliation
and healing
and witnessing.

someone hands me a tissue,
i'm supposed to be crying.

i don't get the answers kokum wants.

there is medicine that grows
by the muskeg
it has a twin
that is poisonous.

"grandma, this lady gave me a 1-800 number
for you to call," my weak words delivering her
non-answers.

kokum says:
she has called
my mom has called

my aunty has called
that dead end.

swampland doesn't heal
it regenerates
and makes the dead
anew.

they destroyed the residential school
at île-à-la-crosse
or so i read in the news.

i carry my ancestors
in my body
and my body
isn't so different
than muskeg:
full of frost
but supporting life.

strong enough to hold
the growth of others
but deep enough
to swallow
spirits whole.

we carry the past
in our dna
we hold its traumas
and its love.

and we pass that down in blood
that has been boiling for 150 years.

wanisinowin

for all our relatives taken too soon

here are some lies i've told today:
i'm fine
it's okay
white people never understand what i mean
when i say:
"but they're my family."

maybe it's because they grew up kicking anthills.

it's not hard
to mourn a stranger
when these strangers aren't so different
from the faces at home.

i'm fine
it's okay

she laughs when i say i can smell the seasons change
but we wake up to frosty mornings caught in
low sunlight.
the birds know it will snow soon,
the leaves are starting to point down.

autumn brings grief and the end of
huckleberries,
it brings longer nights and brighter moons.

the northern lights are stairways to a final home
and they've been dancing a long dance

making room in constellations for souls to rest.

there's a particular heartache we feel,

they probably don't feel it.

but there's a particular heartache we feel
when the river is being dragged
when back roads are being searched
when footprints disappear in snow.

ceremony

for matt and chloe, creator is always watching

hold the braid like this,
here, use this to light it.

we're not supposed to use a lighter?
shit, just use it anyways.
is it going?

okay.

you rub your hands together like this?
push the smoke down your body.

are we doing this right?
how can we tell if we are doing it right?

clumsy, we fumble through a teaching
we were never taught
fingers getting tangled in smoke.

is this a cleansing?
maybe this is a forgetting ceremony –
early morning,
still awake,
last cigarette in the pack.

this is my offering.

touch your spine.
is it there?

touch your lungs.
are they okay?
now pull out your ribcage.

cut your hair and weave a mat with the strands.
stretch your skin over your bones and enter
your shelter.

light a fire, never let it go out.

give 'em hell, iskwew

for lori blondeau

kokum says that vicks can cure all.

she tells me this
as she takes her nightly dollop,
rubs my back with it,
and says the lord's prayer.

Lori, i don't think they know what it's like to
have everything only to have it taken away.
stuck between the burden of representation
and the burden of wanting to be represented
what does it even mean to "be a good woman"?

in kokum's purse there are:
- old receipts
- a half-empty jar of vicks
- a st. christopher medallion
- old phone numbers
- and her sugar pills

in kokum's purse there's no pressure to perform
expectations handed down from introduced
standards.

Lori, dancing with Patsy is a traditional
coming-of-age ceremony that these
moniyawak will never understand.

Lori, you remind me of my mom and aunties:
black-leather jackets with the fringe
big teased hair, red lips, and gold hoops.

getting ready to go out
go to the bar
go to bingo
carrying the burden of being young
of being a woman
of being âpihtaw'ko'sân from sâkitawâhk in
their back pockets.

in kokum's purse she has the same shade of red
lipstick that mom wears
she applies a heavy layer
and kisses a tissue to blot
places it back into her bag.

red lips left like a fingerprint.

Lori, i think kokum has room
in her purse for all of us.

so even when they take it all away,
we have a place to hide that smells like vicks, white
diamonds eau de toilette, and cigarette smoke.

we have a place that can hold us and all these
expectations we weren't expecting.

follow your traplines home

if sadness is a legacy so is joy
    —SELINA BOAN (2021)

we carry the grief of our ancestors.

while we carry
our mothers' grief
our aunties' grief
and the grief of the old woman
we saw in shoppers.

she has a face like our kokums'.

the communion of wrinkles gathered in the
corners of her eyes, dug deep into brown skin:
from laughing
crying
fighting
and loving us through existence.

her wrinkles sprawl like river deltas
like forest trails
like northern logging roads
like traplines.

this being is lonely and full
we exist in the embodied pressure of
what it means *to be*.

it feels like there's an inevitable sadness and we
are just waiting for the levee to break.

what more can they expect from us?
when with each passing day it feels like
we are either reading
or writing
our obituaries.

solace comes in small waves,
and never all at once.

it's the warmth of a lover's palm,
joyful moments in the sun,
over steeped red rose tea.

it's prairie laughter
crinkling up the corners of our eyes
creating traplines for each other
to follow home.

nêwo

kîskatinâw interlude pt. II

I am, as you,   made of water
—MARILYN DUMONT (1996)

she never apologizes.

takes you as an offering,
and continues to flow just as she
did the day before
and the day before that.

i have watched my body ebb and flow
fold, expand,
and consume itself whole.

broken bones and boiled blood:
i have woven
myself together.

how much tendon
and hide does it take
to make a new skin?

i wish there were a better way to say
that i am jealous of a river.

it's hard not to fall in love
with the way she tears away at her banks
and rises with the ice melt each spring.

i know it's in my best interest to be as soft
as her water but i have never been gifted the
ability to be so carefree.

i wish my edges
were soft
like hers.

she calls to me.

she pulls me closer.

counting teeth

i have tangled my fingers
in the hair of others
searching for signs of life.

i have followed capillaries
on the backs of arms
like a map.

this skin is where i call home,
but this skin has been loved
and unloved
into oblivion.

i miss the sound of snow
falling on snow.

the tragedy of love
is the hours spent
lost in my own mind.

i tell myself
i can survive
this wanting hunger.

this body
is not a site of ideal desire.

it is a never-ending battle
and refusal
yet its existence is proof
of my resistance.

this body,
borrowed from the stars,
holds ancient memories
of stories whispered to
snow falling on pine trees.

i will find my way back
to the hole in the sky
by counting the teeth of lovers.

askîy

i have bent myself backwards
trying to find a place for myself
inside of being beautiful.

i have:
broken fingers,
snapped tendons,
made myself smaller,
hoping to be unnoticed
and noticed.

but with this much history
under my skin
i have never been
small enough
to remain hidden.

maybe there's too much
historical hurt
and anger.

please understand
that anger
and love
are intertwined.

there is a reason
we burn
winter-dead brush in the spring.

we were never taught
how to ask someone
to help carry our bones
when they feel too heavy.

we were given
the sinew
to sew ourselves
back together
and keep moving
because the frost is setting in
and we need to set up camp.

this body is not an apology
yet it's been apologizing
since time immemorial
for loneliness
and transgressions
it doesn't understand.

rivers flood valleys
to create new life
this land has never been
interested in being
small.

kiyâm

you are more than pretty.
you are infinite.
you are huckleberries and moose meat.
comparing yourself to white girls is an
inevitable means to an end when you were
raised with survival instead of sweetness.
my name is roogaroo.
my name is wîhtikow.

somewhere along the dreams of my mothers,
these stories got intertwined.

they were a warning,
and not a guide
on how to find myself.

"the skill set you need to survive is not the
same skill set you need to love and be loved."
i write myself into existence
but my existence is lost to words
that i can't translate into english
so i exist in the space between every
mispronounced syllable of my stolen tongue.

he's sitting across the table and this is the last
time i'll see him.
my memories will exist in my daughters'
dreams and their daughters' dreams and their
daughters' dreams.
just like my mothers' exist in mine.

we remember this particular vulnerability
across generations.
breaking this wide open is what got me into
this mess, and in my blood, i hope future
generations know their strength comes in
walking away before waiting for the apology.
i will sew porcupine quills onto my hands to
stop history from repeating.
acceptance and admitting defeat are not
med'cines i've been gifted.

nothing is ever simple

i have only had one honest one-night stand.

we met for drinks, but he was straight edge
so i drank two americanos
and we bought candy
and went back to his place.

intimacy is an ephemeral thing.

making out during a david lynch movie
felt so on-brand for twenty-three.

i could tell by the way the night was going
neither of us were into each other
but we were into
not being alone
and the affirmation of kissing.

emptiness is a space
two people
can fill.

i sneak out to avoid his roommate.

see comics on the coffee table
mid-century modern accents
decorate his basement suite

we are all broke
and we are all worried about aesthetics.

on the cab ride home
i promise my ancestors
that i will never write the words:
"straight-edge vegan one-night stand"
again.

i bend down and stick my hands into the dirt,
grab a fistfull and pull it close:

inhale.

this coastal dirt smells different.

the knowledge i have from surviving northern
winters has helped me in this city
but i still dream of whisky jacks
and grandpa's alarm clock
roaring the cbc at 6 a.m.

if you lie on your back
along the sukunka
you can see every star.

this is where dad
pointed and said:

"that's the north star. if you're ever lost
you can follow her home."

i can't tell my one-night stand
that i know there are more than four seasons.

one-time lovers
can't follow me back
to the beginning.

only goodbye
and a sloppy kiss
send me off into the night.

nothing is simple here, m'girl.

more muskrat

i have been cutting my hair
for the last five years
it's my own sort-of-mourning ceremony.

there's an untold origin story
about the bodies
of halfbreed girls:
we are where the world begins and ends,
we are more muskrat than girl.

i trace the words i will never say to him
into thin air with the tip of my tongue
never able to tease out the fact
that he's more unstable than a cutbank.

at grandma's there's a hill
where my brother used to bury dead birds.

my family named the hill after me,
this is my naming ceremony: dead-bird girl.

i ask aunty if this is my creation story.

underneath my skin you can follow
my veins like ski-doo trails
back to where my first ancestor laid her head.

under his skin the path is much less travelled.

this world could start again
yet he forgets that he's not the centre of where

this earth comes from
he's not even a mark on her surface.

i am scared that if i let my hair grow long
i won't be able to hide that my body is more
story than physics:
full of feathers and tadpoles.

"i keep meaning to ask you,
what's it like to be a bearberry?"

aunty, how do you say unrequited in our language?

wash your hair;
stand in the shower
and turn the water as hot
as your skin will take.

accidently let your hand brush theirs.

count the seconds
until you have your first intrusive thought
count the seconds
until you have your
second
third
fourth.

don't touch reality until your next shower.

stretch your skin until it's tight
make a rattle with your bones.

you don't ask the ancestors for much
but maybe you will for this.

loneliness is an apology,
so let go
loudly.

understand the irony of chasing moniyâw nâpewak
laugh until your lungs hurt.

is this a ceremony?

continuously look for hope
in dilated pupils
get lost.

follow the north star home
find the wrong constellation
on purpose.

you missed the lesson
about the impossibility of
loving someone until they love
you the way you want them to.

mourn.
grieve.

make friends with the cîpay that find you at night

gather pine boughs
and goose down.

make your bed.

trickster

while he dreams of me,
i leave strands of hair on his pillow.

in my dreams
he leaves pieces of himself
that whisper half-formed promises.

i ask the night if love is a trickster.

i want to hold his hand
under the migrating moon
instead i hold all our unsaid words.

soft and heavy,
they fit perfectly between my fingers.

they are our creation story
and i am my own trickster.

i ask him,
"please breathe
the human
back into me."

i ask for too much.

i can't beg him to witness
the buffalo returning.

he never sees me
as endless yellow canola in late august.

this is where his end begins.

i ask him,
"what does it mean to be ready?"

i ask the night:
"kîḵwêy kiwâpahtîn?"

it's berry-picking season now,
the huckleberries are ripe
up on grizzly ridge.

i've never had to ask
the berry bush if they're ready,
we have a perfect understanding:

i take only what i need
and in return
the berry bush sees me
as prairie grass
and wholly human.

pahkwêsikan

"aunty, what do i do
when he doesn't love me back?"

"add butter to flour, sammy"

"aunty, how do i
crawl inside
your ribcage?"

"add milk slowly"

"aunty, he left me for a white girl."

"remember to always add a pinch of sugar"

"aunty, what do i do
when moving on feels like regret?"

"mix the batter with your hands until it feels
like sand sliding through your fingers"

"aunty, why wasn't his love
a revolution?"

"remember to never over-knead your dough"

"aunty, how do i find myself?"

"if you over-knead your dough, sammy, it will
get tough"

"aunty, i am scared of being over-kneaded."

"heat oil slowly, baby girl"

"aunty, why are these memories lingering in my bedroom?"

"if you heat the oil too fast, sammy, it will smoke. you can't use oil if it starts to smoke"

"aunty, i'm being haunted."

"we cut the dough like this so it cooks evenly"

"aunty, what is decolonization?"

"fry till light brown"

"aunty, how do i say no?"

"serve warm"

"aunty, i love you."

"with butter or lard and honey"

"aunty, how do frogs survive the winter?"

bluebells

"did you taste
the sweet nectar of bluebells
that lingers under my tongue?"

every day i watch people stop and smell the
flowers in my front yard
small pleasures dance across their faces
in the middle of disaster.

all I can think of is how much i want to kiss the
inside of his neck.
i'm a half-formed lapsed catholic confessional
here for him to whisper all his secrets to.

a woman stops to take a picture of the shadow
my house casts on the warehouse across the
street:
i am in love with her.
for his sins, it will be five halfbreed hail marys:

> dip your feet in the ceremonial waters at lac
> ste. anne, but only if they're not poisoned
> by cyanobacteria blooms, thriving in settler
> waste from lakeside cottages.

i keep wondering if i
will ever get sick of writing about endings.

or dreaming about my ending
and predicting our ending.

when do i become fully formed?
if all he sees
is an amalgamation of everything
he wants to see.

for him i was never
winter and warning stories.

that'll be another trip
to another confessional.

"tell her what you saw of me."

standards

i'm sick of writing poems
about my body
for you.

hoping that if i
compare my breasts
to rolling hills
and my hips to curvy rivers
you will see in me
the land i come from.

i've lost my way
trying to find a place
inside of beautiful
for you.

i weave together
lines of poetry
so i can wrap myself
in your existence.

but the spirit
held in the soft
homeland of my body
speaks to me in dreams:

"m'girl,
you're the lake,
and the shore,
and the sunlight
on a quiet afternoon.

you're a part of a whole,
sent here to learn
how to be delicately
human."

niyânan

my body remembers

i met him when i was 20.

belly up on my too-small dorm bed,
he told me that he could take
whatever he wanted:

                                    and he did.

my spine stiffened
as i washed him off my sheets
and turned him into a funny story.

laughter hiding what my spine knew.

laughter hiding why i cried
the next time
someone was in my bed.

in my body
i have hidden secrets in the empty spaces
between my ribs.

when i left at 13
he leaned through the truck window
and said:
"you can never come back."

vertebrae telling me
that coming back
was never an option.

my spine is my greatest love story
each bone coming to attention
to warn me
hold me
pick me back up.

i have held my softness
between my teeth
and my resistance in every intervertebral disc.

i have felt my spine soften,
guard down at a first kiss.

backbone coming undone to show me that she
knows when i can safely lay bare.

she keeps me stable
remembers how to shake
with enough laughter
to heal us both.

nâwikan, this is a story of my love for you
and for the ways you whisper
through our body to remind me:

it is in my best interest
        to be very tender.

wildfire

i disintegrate beside her
make myself small
laugh quieter.

my kokum told me
we come from a family of dreamers.

she tells me this after i dream
of long-ago relatives
speaking to me in my sleep.

after my great-aunt's funeral in meadow lake
i wake up on kokum's couch
with my family around me
a portrait of my aunt
tucked under my pillow.

they search for reason
in this mystery.

in my dreams
i ignore what the spirits tell
me about her:
"run away m'girl
            and never look back."

i reach within myself
pull a new skin over my body,
one that is translucent
and agreeable.

i twist my bones to stay in her orbit
i have more to lose
if i don't turn my insides out.

some people burn like wildfires
fast and bright,
destroying everything in their path.

yet in their wake,
wildfires make room
for new life.

in my dreams
i watch fireweed grow out of burnt tree trunks
watch my friends turn beautiful
as the ash settles.

my see-through skin
soaks up the sun,
and i am made anew.

my ghost stays in my body

After great pain, a formal feeling comes –
—EMILY DICKINSON (1862)

these warm coastal winters have been lulling
me into a deceitful complacency; 21 felt so old
but that was many different iterations of "ya
but it's a wet cold" ago and now i don't even
bother telling strangers i'm from the north.

The Nerves sit ceremonious, like Tombs –
The stiff Heart questions "was it He, that bore,"
And "Yesterday, or Centuries before"?

i learned to talk to strangers in coded secrets
wrapped in my birth chart:
"i'm a capricorn" is code for "i'm an unfeeling bitch."
"i'm a double taurus" is code for "i'm a lazy,
cold, hedonistic bitch." my rising and moon
change depending on what app i am using:
some say i'm an aquarius rising, with a taurus
moon. which is code for "i'm a cold, dreamy,
hedonistic bitch."
"i'm a sagittarius venus."
i hope that this will be enough reasoning for why i
am detached until I'm not. i want it to explain why
i fall in and out of love with each heartbeat.

i wonder when we will stop using astrology to
explain away our worst parts.

The Feet, mechanical, go round –
A Wooden way
Of Ground, or Air, or Ought –
Regardless grown,
A Quartz contentment, like a stone –

how many more times do i have to wrap myself
in tender loving words before i feel loving and
tender? my therapist agrees that i should start
recording what happens when i disassociate.

in session – neither of us have used the word
disassociate, dancing around its implications.

instead, i say:
"i feel myself leave my body. i feel the fog roll in
and i watch myself from the corner of the room."

somewhere i read that we are bones inside a
meat sack controlled by a ghost. i wonder, as
i'm watching myself from the corner of the
ceiling, if that's my ghost taking a break.

i leave my body when i hear someone raise
their voice, when i tell people i love them,
when people are kind.
maybe it's not that i'm a capricorn cold
unfeeling bitch, maybe my ghost has unionized
and gets to take 10-to-15-minute breaks every
couple hours.

i tell my therapist i've been pushing myself to
tell people i care about them.

i start small with a:
"i like spending time with you," followed by
replying to months-old messages. followed by
hugging more.

my ghost stays in my body.

First – Chill – then Stupor – then the letting go –

turner st.,

i can change,
i can change, i can change,
i can –.

for L,

i tried to make this one rhyme
because you love a rhyming poem
but i couldn't make it work.

trauma is breaking apart
and spending the rest of your life
trying to collect the pieces
this is my birthright.

i just didn't mean
for you to have
a front-row seat.

do you remember
when we first spent time together?
drinking vodka from the bottle
listening to our only two records.

we wandered around campus
looking for cigarettes
looking for the night
pine-cone bees hanging from trees
marking our path back home.

ten years is a long time
but not that long.

i'll be front row at your show.

i'm thankful
that in my life
i've had a love like you.

do you remember
when we got into that fight in chinatown?
late-night laughter
replaced with something else
the reason we were fighting is not important
or maybe it is
but mistakes are hard to negotiate.

you were there to watch my ends fray
and help me braid them into something new.

the urge to split my differences
and take the back road out
comes naturally to me.

it's another birthright.

you tell me not to
that my existence matters in yours
and i don't believe you because
my existence is unexpected
and –

do you remember every joke?
"we are the funniest people in this city"
we say this, again and again.

i believe it.

this is reading like a love poem
because it is.

my friend
you are one of my greatest loves
in this perpetually ending world.

in this city
that i've been navigating
with my shoes on the wrong feet
you fended off the bears.

i keep saying:
"i want what's best for you."

we continue
to take chances on strangers
have more coffee
more laughter
i will dry your hair
while you help me walk through this life
with my left shoe
on my right foot.

nikotwâsik

mclean drive,

i break loose in isolation
crashing upon the rocks of myself.

i cry for two weeks straight
only stopping for sleep
and water.

long lessons learned
the hard way:
we are only loved
the way spring loves
fresh flowers.

even in endings,
there is renewal.

i break open myself,
to form new rivers.

mwîstas kakî wâpam'tin?

saint

how many times did we have to hold
each other's hands
through living?

the underbelly of a fish is its most tender place
you – fish belly – are mine
and i think that's what's made
this growing so painful.

you were the only motherfucker
in this city who knew how to handle me.

where the sun touches my body

i dream that
the sun is my
fat-bodied kin
    —DALLAS HUNT (2021)

as the sun
meets the horizon
at the break of dawn
i wonder if he notices
the moment before he touches the land.

the juncture between two moments
makes forgetting an act of remembering.

what do you call dreams
that feel like memories?

i long to be longed for,
or at least told that i am.

the space between dream
and reality
is a lonely buffer zone,
yet i exist there, persistently.

my dream world forms
in the middle of my waking day.

while there,
i turn sternums into gardens
to grow all my plants.

uproot my favourite parts to see
if there are bits of me
growing in the soil.

like lifting up rocks
to uncover crabs on the beach,
like disturbing a house
to find a home.

i exist
in the moment between
the sun's decision to set
and his goodbye.

i'll hold my own hand and yours

jessica says ceremony is:

"wanting to have two wives
& one husband
& filling them all with so much love
they feel it in the webs
of their feet"

this ceremony,
i braid my hair for.

my fingertips trace
the uneven paths of your palm
while your fingertips
write manifestos on my stomach.

i tell myself that whatever happens, happens.

despite all that i have weathered
i can survive getting lost
in someone else's storm.

i whisper my secrets to the black spruce
greying in the muskeg,
they are aging aunties
cared for by time.

i learn to love
by watching snow fall on snow
hoping that it's as gentle,
beautiful,
and silent.

i'm scared to say what i really think:
you're a wonderful mess,
a tangle alfalfa on the side of the highway.

my lips are always
pointing to the horizon
anticipating collapse.

between our bodies
is space
that only time can fill.

jessica says:

"be careful
let it be beautiful
& pay attention,"

and i think i'll listen to her.

chickadee

chickadee watches the end of each season
and lovingly sings us into the next.
she watches a thousand little deaths
and a thousand more little births
before she sees hers.

one being's apocalypse is another's
good morning.

aren't we all just the representation
of many beginnings and endings?

for me to be here
the world had to begin
    and end
êkwa kâh-kîhtwâm.

i dream of aunties i've never met,
sitting around kokum's table,
northern wind escaping their lips,
they tell me that my first love has to be
continuation.

from her branch outside my window,
chickadee reminds me of the good memories.

grandma taught me
how to listen
to her.

chickadee teaches me lessons on grief
and the tenderness of existence.

she reminds me to hold onto every small
pleasure:

the softness of the morning
the warmth of summer nights
someone's hand in yours,
and heavy august sunlight
dancing across the kitchen table.

she carries the weight of the world
only to tell us:

"the certainty of an end
makes room for us
to begin again,

and again,

and again."

ACKNOWLEDGMENTS

these poems were written on the unceded Lands of the xʷməθkʷəy̓əm, Sḵwx̱wú7mesh, and səlilwətaɬ. i am deeply grateful to be able to learn all these lessons here.

many of these poems talk about my love and respect for being raised by the Land in the bc peace region. i have deep gratitude for the love of my Treaty 8 kin. i want to acknowledge my northern prairie Homelands. i call upon them in many different ways through these poems despite not living there. i am grateful to be loved by them through time and space.

this book is a love song to my mom. i love you mom, thank you for everything. it is also an unending love letter to my grandma on the farm, my kokum, and my aunty rita. thank you all for forming me into the person i am today. thank you to my brother for being my biggest support and best friend. thank you dad for bringing the gift of poetry into my life and nurturing my creativity. i love you more than words. thank you everyone in my family for holding me in so many beautiful ways.

thank you cecily nicholson for your guidance through the editing process, i am so thankful for the care and love you showed this body of work. thank you mercedes eng for getting the ball rolling on this whole thing. i am in such awe and appreciation to everyone in the writing community who has nurtured and guided me with such care.

i am so incredibly blessed to have such a glorious constellation of people in my life who show me such unrelenting love. thank you lindsay m for being my soulmate northern cuzzin in this city. thank you myles for showing me such a beautiful love. thank you lindsay s for learning and growing with me through our messy and wonderful 20s, and thank you tylar, michal, alie, dan, and everyone else who has loved me through these years.

matt and chloe, thank you for being the constants in this wild life. i love you both so much. this book wouldn't be here without you.

i am only one part of a much larger solar system of incredible Indigenous talent: thank you jess for being the first set of eyes on this book and thank you brandi for your guidance and care. i also want to acknowledge the brilliance and wisdom of salia, anna, erica violet lee, dallas, emily, billy-ray, and so many others; how lucky am i to have too many people to thank and not enough space to do it?

thank you daniel heath justice, who so many years ago through a skype call told me that my dream of this book would be possible.

thank you charles and the team at talonbooks for being such a welcoming home for this work.

lastly, thank you reader for joining me on this journey.

SOURCES

"follow your traplines home"
Selina Boan, "have you ever fallen in love with a day," *Undoing Hours* (Gibsons, BC: Nightwood Editions, 2021), 74.

"kîskatinâw interlude pt. II"
Marilyn Dumont, "We Are Made of Water," *A Really Good Brown Girl* (London, ON: Brick Books, 1996), 77.

"kiyâm"
Leanne Betasamosake Simpson, "Buffalo On," *Islands of Decolonial Love: Stories & Songs* (Winnipeg: ARP Books, 2013), 86.

"my ghost stays in my body"
Emily Dickinson, "After great pain, a formal feeling comes –" (1862), *The Poems of Emily Dickinson: Reading Edition*, edited by R.W. Franklin (Cambridge, MA, and London, UK: Belknap Press of Harvard University Press, 1999), 170. Online: Poetry Foundation, www.poetryfoundation.org/poems/47651/after-great-pain-a-formal-feeling-comes-372.

"where the sun touches my body"
Dallas Hunt, "Stretch Marks // Sun Dogs," *Creeland* (Gibsons, BC: Nightwood Editions, 2021), 52.

"i'll hold my own hand and yours"
Jessica Johns, "Nehiyaw Iskwewak," *How Not to Spill* (Vancouver: Rahila's Ghost Press, 2018), 38.

SAMANTHA NOCK is an âpihtaw'kos'ân writer and poet
from Treaty 8 Territory in the Peace Region of northeast
British Columbia. Her family is originally from sâkitawâk
(Île-à-la-Crosse), Saskatchewan. Samantha currently
resides on unceded xʷməθkʷəẏəm, Sḵwx̱wú7mesh, and
səlilwətaɬ Lands in so-called Vancouver. She has had works
published in *Maisonneuve, Vice, Prism International,* and
Best Canadian Poetry, among others. You can find her on
Twitter @sammymarie and Instagram @2broke4bingo.